FOREX TRADING FUNDAMENTALS

A PRACTICAL GUIDE TO UNDERSTANDING THE BASICS OF FOREX MARKETS, CURRENCY PAIRS AND HOW FOREX TRADING WORKS FOR BEGINNERS AND PROFESSIONALS

EXPLOIT KNOWLEDGE

Copyright©2024 EXPLOIT KNOWLEDGE

All Rights Reserved

ISBN: 9798324787899

Contact:

+2348030720719

Exploitnneka@gmail.com

TABLE OF CONTENT

TABLE OF CONTENT 2

PREFACE 13

INTRODUCTION TO THE BOOK 13
WHAT TO EXPECT 13
HOW TO USE THIS BOOK 14
MY PERSONAL JOURNEY IN FOREX 14

CHAPTER 1 16

INTRODUCTION TO FOREX TRADING 16
WHAT EXACTLY IS FOREX TRADING? 16
BRIEF HISTORY OF FOREX MARKETS 17
SIGNIFICANCE OF FOREX TRADING IN THE GLOBAL ECONOMY ... 18

CHAPTER 2 20

UNDERSTANDING THE STRUCTURE OF FOREX MARKETS ... 20
OVERVIEW OF THE FOREX MARKET 20
Central Banks: 21
Major Commercial Banks: 22

Governments and International Organizations 22

Corporations 23

Different Categories of the Forex Market: Spot, Forward, and Futures 23

Forward Market: 24

Futures Market: 24

CHAPTER 3   26

UNDERSTANDING CURRENCY PAIRS   26

Understanding Currency Pairs 26

Major Pairs, Minor Pairs, and Exotic Pairs 27

Minor Pairs: 27

Exotic Pairs: 28

Understanding the Mechanics of Currency Pairs 28

Analysis of Fundamentals: 29

Technical Analysis: 29

CHAPTER 4   31

READING FOREX QUOTES   31

Understanding the Structure of Forex Quotes 31

Understanding Bid and Ask Prices 32

Market Price: 32

Ask Price (or Offer Price): 32

The selling price 32

UNDERSTANDING PIPS, POINTS, AND SPREADS 33
Pips: 33
Spreads: 34

CHAPTER 5 36

FUNDAMENTAL CONCEPTS IN FOREX 36
BASE AND QUOTE CURRENCIES 36
UNDERSTANDING LOT SIZE AND ITS IMPACT ON INVESTMENTS 37
Lot Size: 37
THREE MAIN TYPES OF LOT SIZES EXIST: 37
Standard Lot: 37
Mini Lot: 37
Leverage: 38
Margin 39

CHAPTER 6 41

HOW FOREX TRADING WORKS 41
THE MECHANICS OF FOREX TRADING 41
EXECUTING A FOREX TRADE 42
Choose the Type of Trade: 42
Choose the size of your lot: 43
Consider Utilizing Leverage: 43
Establish Stop Loss and Take Profit Levels: 43

Execute the Trade:	44
EXPLORING DIFFERENT ORDER TYPES	44
Market Order:	44
Limit Order:	45
Stop-Loss Order:	45
Profit Locking Order:	46
Stop-Entry Order:	46

CHAPTER 7 — 48

ANALYZING THE FOREX MARKET — 48

FUNDAMENTAL ANALYSIS	48
KEY ECONOMIC INDICATORS	49
GDP (Gross Domestic Product):	49
Employment Data:	49
Trade Balance:	49
Interest rates:	50
ECONOMIC THEORIES THAT DRIVE FOREX	50
Purchasing Power Parity (PPP)	51
Interest Rate Parity	51
Balance of Payments Model:	51
TECHNICAL ANALYSIS	52
DIFFERENT TYPES OF CHARTS	52
Line charts	52
Candlestick Charts:	53

IMPORTANT TECHNICAL INDICATORS	54
Moving Averages:	54
RSI (Relative Strength Index)	54
MACD (Moving Average Convergence Divergence):	55
UNDERSTANDING SUPPORT AND RESISTANCE	55
Support:	55
Resistance:	55
CHAPTER 8	**57**
DEVELOPING A TRADING PLAN	**57**
IMPORTANCE OF HAVING A TRADING PLAN	57
COMPONENTS OF AN EFFECTIVE TRADING STRATEGY	58
Setting Trading Goals:	58
Risk/Reward Ratio:	58
Criteria for Entering and Exiting Trades:	58
Money Management Rules:	59
Market Analysis:	59
Effective Record Keeping:	59
RISK MANAGEMENT STRATEGIES	60
Stop-Loss Orders:	60
Position Sizing:	60
Embrace diversification:	60
Effective Management of Leverage:	60
Consistent Evaluations:	61

CHAPTER 9   63

COMMON FOREX TRADING STRATEGIES   63
EXPLORING THE WORLD OF FOREX DAY TRADING   63
Market Hours: 63
Speed and Precision: 64
Risk Management: 64
Technical Analysis: 64
EFFECTIVE STRATEGIES FOR SWING TRADING   64
Timing: 65
Technical and Fundamental Analysis: 65
Risk Tolerance: 65
Persistence and Patience: 66
POSITION TRADING: EMBRACING A STRATEGIC APPROACH   66
Fundamental Focus: 67
Market Sentiment and Trends: 67
Managing Risk: 67
Resilience: 67

CHAPTER 10   69

TOOLS OF THE TRADE   69
FOREX TRADING PLATFORMS   69
MetaTrader 4 and 5 (MT4/MT5):   69
cTrader: 70

NinjaTrader:	70
Thinkorswim:	70
TOOLS FOR ANALYSIS	71
Charting Software:	71
Exploring Technical Indicators and Oscillators:	72
Sentiment indicators	72
A COMPUTERIZED TRADING SYSTEMS	72
Efficiency:	73
Discipline:	73
Backtesting:	73
Over-Optimization:	73

CHAPTER 11 — 75

UNDERSTANDING THE PSYCHOLOGY OF TRADING — 75

UNDERSTANDING THE PSYCHOLOGICAL FACTORS IN TRADING	75
PSYCHOLOGICAL FACTORS IMPACTING FOREX TRADERS	76
Overconfidence Bias:	76
Confirmation Bias:	76
Loss Aversion:	77
Anchoring Bias:	77
BUILDING MENTAL DISCIPLINE	77
Establishing Clear Objectives:	78
Developing and adhering to a well-structured trading strategy:	78
Effective Stress Management:	78

Consistent Evaluation and Contemplation: 79

Maintaining a Trading Journal: 79

CHAPTER 12 — 81

NAVIGATING RISKS IN FOREX TRADING — 81

POTENTIAL RISKS INVOLVED IN FOREX TRADING — 81

Risk of Leverage: 82

Interest rate risk: 82

Risk of Limited Liquidity: 82

Political and Economic Risk: 82

STRATEGIES TO MITIGATE RISKS — 83

Utilizing Stop-Loss Orders: 83

Appropriate Leverage Use: 83

Understanding Risk/Reward Ratios: 84

Diversification: 84

Hedging: 84

THE SIGNIFICANCE OF ONGOING EDUCATION — 85

Educational Resources: 85

Economic Calendars and News Outlets: 85

Simulation and Backtesting: 86

Become part of trading communities: 86

CHAPTER 13 — 87

LEGAL AND REGULATORY ENVIRONMENT   87

REGULATIONS FOR FOREX TRADING   87

In the United Kingdom,   88

Within the European Union,   88

UNDERSTANDING YOUR RIGHTS AND RESPONSIBILITIES   89

Rights: 89

Responsibilities: 89

PROTECTING YOURSELF FROM SCAMS AND FRAUDS   90

Verify Broker Credentials: 90

Be Wary of Unrealistic Promises: 90

Research Thoroughly: 91

Use Secure and Transparent Payment Methods: 91

Educate Yourself Continuously: 91

LEGAL REMEDIES AND PROCEDURES FOR ADDRESSING COMPLAINTS   92

APPENDIX   94

ONLINE COURSES   94

1. Babypips: 94
2. Udemy: 94
3. Coursera and EdX: 94
4. To access our online course after purchasing this book send an email to: 95

WEBSITES   95

1. Investopedia: 95

2.	Forex Factory:	95
3.	DailyFX:	95

TOOLS 95

1.	Economic Calendars:	95
2.	Demo Accounts:	96
3.	Trading Platforms:	96

FORUMS AND SOCIAL MEDIA 96

1.	Forex Reddit Community (r/Forex):	96
2.	Trading View:	96
3.	Bloomberg Market Concepts (BMC):	96

MOBILE APPS 97

1.	Thinkorswim:	97
2.	FXStreet:	97
3.	Bloomberg Business Mobile App:	97

EPILOGUE   **98**

Looking Ahead	99
Embracing Continuous Improvement	99
The Role of Persistence	100
Final Thoughts	101

NOTE TO FX TRADERS   **102**

PREFACE

Introduction to the Book

Welcome to this book where I provide valuable insights that, if implemented correctly, can greatly enhance your trading journey. As you hold this book in your hands, you're about to embark on an exhilarating journey into the ever-evolving realm of Forex trading. Whether you're new to the world of forex trading or have years of experience under your belt, this book is designed to be your go-to resource for all things related to the market.

What to Expect

In this book, my goal is to simplify the intricacies of Forex trading and give you a strong basis to begin your trading journey. Whether you're new to the world of trading or seeking to expand your knowledge, you'll discover valuable insights, practical advice, and effective strategies to improve your trading abilities.

How to Use This Book

To fully benefit from this book, I suggest viewing it as a guide rather than a final destination. Every chapter progresses from the previous one, leading you from the fundamentals of Forex markets to more intricate concepts and strategies. Feel free to take your time to fully understand the information, actively participate in the exercises and examples given, and feel confident in revisiting chapters whenever necessary.

My Personal Journey in Forex

My own journey in Forex trading began with curiosity and a desire to understand the financial markets better. Like many beginners, I encountered challenges and setbacks along the way, but I persevered, learning from both successes and failures. Through dedication, continuous learning, and the support of mentors and fellow traders, I've been able to navigate the complexities of Forex trading and achieve consistent results.

As I share my knowledge and experiences with you in this book, I hope to empower you on your own journey to trading success. Remember, Forex trading is not just about making profits; it's a journey of self-discovery, discipline, and growth.

I wish you the best of luck on your Forex trading journey and hope that this book serves as a valuable companion along the way.

Happy trading!

Your Exploit is my Concern

CHAPTER 1

INTRODUCTION TO FOREX TRADING

What exactly is Forex Trading?

Foreign exchange, or forex, is all about trading different currencies against each other. The forex market boasts an impressive daily volume of over $6 trillion, making it the largest financial market globally. Participants include a wide range of entities, from large financial institutions and multinational corporations to individual retail traders. Participants in forex trading can exchange currencies required for foreign trade and investment. Traders aim to make profits by speculating on the future direction of forex prices, capitalizing on changes in the value of one currency against another.

Brief History of Forex Markets

The practice of trading currencies has been around for centuries, dating back to the origins of different forms of currency. In the past, currencies were exchanged through a barter system. However, as economies and monetary systems became more sophisticated, the demand for a standardized currency exchange became evident. The forex market started to take shape in the 1970s when several countries transitioned from fixed to floating exchange rates after the breakdown of the Bretton Woods Agreement in 1971. This signaled a shift away from the previously limited and controlled trading within certain government-regulated markets to a worldwide decentralized market that operates around the clock, five days a week.

Significance of Forex Trading in the Global Economy

Understanding the ins and outs of forex trading is essential for successfully navigating the world of international business and trade. In today's highly interconnected world, the seamless exchange of currencies is crucial for the smooth functioning of global operations. As an example, when a company in the United States wants to import goods from Japan, it usually has to carry out the transaction in yen. This means that the U.S. Company needs to convert its dollars into Japanese yen. In addition to trade, forex trading plays a crucial role in maintaining global financial stability. The fluctuation of exchange rates has a significant impact on inflation, the balance of trade, and ultimately, the economies of countries across the globe. In addition, the forex markets have a significant impact on determining currency prices, which in turn influence foreign investment flows, tourism, international mergers and acquisitions, and geopolitical relationships.

By gaining a solid grasp of the fundamentals of forex trading, its historical evolution, and its significant role in the global economy, traders and economists can effectively navigate this expansive and intricate market. This understanding lays the foundation for diving further into the mechanics of forex trading and crafting successful trading strategies.

CHAPTER 2

UNDERSTANDING THE STRUCTURE OF FOREX MARKETS

Overview of the Forex Market

The Forex market, also referred to as the foreign exchange market, operates round the clock, five days a week, facilitating currency trading. In contrast to other financial markets, Forex operates through a vast global network of banks, corporations, and individuals, without a centralized exchange. The decentralized nature of Forex makes it highly accessible and usually very liquid, providing substantial trading volume and market activity. The trading of currencies occurs in pairs, with the value of a currency pair representing the exchange rate between the two currencies. The rate is subject to constant changes due to a range of economic and geopolitical factors, such as interest rates, inflation, and political stability.

Key Players in the Forex Market

The Forex markets are heavily influenced by various important participants, each with their own unique role in determining currency values and providing liquidity. The main participants consist of:

Central Banks: The key players shaping the Forex market. They play a crucial role in managing the supply of national currency and implementing monetary policy, which has a significant impact on the values of currencies. Central banks have the power to directly impact Forex markets through interventions and indirectly through the manipulation of interest rates.

Major Commercial Banks: The interbank market is where the majority of currency transactions take place, with major banks exchanging currencies at wholesale prices. These banks play a crucial role in Forex markets as they act as primary dealers, representing both themselves and their clients.

Governments and International Organizations play a crucial role in the world of currency exchange. They are actively engaged in managing reserves, facilitating international trade payments, and overseeing significant contracts and foreign investments that necessitate currency conversion.

Corporations engage in Forex primarily to hedge and trade, fulfilling their business needs like paying for goods and services abroad or managing revenues received in foreign currencies. Retail traders and investors play a crucial role in the market, despite their smaller volume compared to other participants. Their influence is steadily increasing, thanks to the widespread availability of online trading platforms.

Different Categories of the Forex Market: Spot, Forward, and Futures

There are three distinct types of markets in forex trading:

The spot market is where currencies are bought and sold based on their trading price at that moment. This market is the largest of its kind, thanks to its "real time" nature. It serves as the foundation for the forwards and futures markets, representing the underlying reality. The majority of retail traders participate in the spot market.

Forward Market: In contrast to the spot market, a forward contract involves a confidential arrangement between two parties to purchase or sell a currency at a later date and at a prearranged price in the OTC markets. Many companies use this form of trading to protect them against currency risk.

Futures Market: Comparable to forwards, futures contracts have a crucial distinction - they are legally binding and traded on a centralized exchange. Futures contracts are standardized agreements that determine the amount of currency being exchanged. They are commonly utilized by speculators and investors who seek to protect their other investments or secure prices.

Having a deep understanding of the structure of Forex markets is essential for traders of all levels. Understanding the operations of various market sectors and the key players involved can greatly assist in making well-informed decisions. Having a strong understanding of these fundamental principles is crucial when it comes to successfully navigating the Forex market and crafting advanced trading strategies.

CHAPTER 3

UNDERSTANDING CURRENCY PAIRS

Understanding Currency Pairs

In the world of forex trading, currencies are traded in pairs, with each pair reflecting the exchange rate between two different currencies. These pairs are represented in a standard format, with one currency as the base and another as the quote. The base currency is the currency being bought or sold for the quote currency. It represents the amount of the quote currency required to buy one unit of the base currency. The value of a currency pair is determined by the quantity of the quote currency needed to purchase a single unit of the base currency.

Major Pairs, Minor Pairs, and Exotic Pairs

There are three main types of currency pairs, which are classified based on their trading volume and liquidity:

Major Pairs: These are the most traded currency pairs in the world and include the US Dollar paired with other major currencies. Some examples are EUR/USD, USD/JPY, GBP/USD, and USD/CHF. These currency pairs are highly liquid and typically have narrow spreads due to their popularity among traders and investors.

Minor Pairs: Also known as cross-currency pairs, these do not include the US Dollar. Some examples of minor currency pairs include EUR/GBP, GBP/JPY, and AUD/NZD. They have lower liquidity compared to the major pairs and may have slightly wider spreads.

Exotic Pairs: These pairs involve one major currency and one currency from a smaller or emerging economy, such as USD/SGD (US Dollar/Singapore Dollar) or EUR/TRY (Euro/Turkish Lira). Exotic pairs tend to have lower liquidity and higher spread due to their lower trading volume.

Understanding the Mechanics of Currency Pairs

When engaging in forex trading, individuals participate in the exchange of currencies, buying one while simultaneously selling another. This combination of actions is what creates a currency pair. As an illustration, if you were to purchase the EUR/USD pair, you would be acquiring Euros while exchanging US Dollars. If the Euro strengthens against the Dollar, the price of the pair will increase, allowing you to potentially profit by selling back the pair at the higher price.

Multiple factors contribute to the fluctuation of currency pair prices, such as economic indicators, market sentiment, political events, and central bank decisions.

Traders utilize a combination of fundamental and technical analysis to forecast currency price movements and make informed trading choices.

Analysis of Fundamentals: This entails evaluating economic indicators like GDP growth rates, employment figures, and interest rate decisions, which have the potential to impact currency values.

Technical Analysis: It entails analyzing chart patterns and utilizing technical indicators such as moving averages and stochastic oscillators to forecast future price movements by examining historical market data.

Having a solid grasp of how currency pairs operate is essential for success in the forex market. Understanding the factors that impact the fluctuations of these currency pairs and their underlying structures allows traders to effectively navigate the intricate realm of forex trading and make well-informed choices.

CHAPTER 4

READING FOREX QUOTES

Understanding the Structure of Forex Quotes

Forex quotes illustrate the value of one currency relative to another and are commonly shown in pairs. Take this quote as an example: EUR/USD 1.1205. In this case, the base currency is EUR and the quote currency is USD. The quote indicates that one Euro is equal to 1.1205 US Dollars. There are two prices involved in Forex quotes: the bid and the ask. Having a solid grasp of interpreting these quotes is essential for successful trading.

Understanding Bid and Ask Prices

Market Price: The market price represents the value at which a particular currency pair can be purchased from you by the market or your broker. Therefore, it is at this price that you, as a trader, have the opportunity to sell the base currency. Usually, it tends to be lower than the ask price.

Ask Price (or Offer Price): The ask price represents the amount at which the market is willing to sell the currency pair to you. This indicates the price at which you have the opportunity to purchase the base currency.

The selling price is consistently higher than the buying price. The spread, which represents the broker's profit from the trade, is determined by the difference between these two prices. It also reflects the liquidity of the currency pair, aside from any commission or fees involved.

Understanding Pips, Points, and Spreads

Pips: A pip represents a small fluctuation in the exchange rate between two currencies. Typically, a pip represents a small fraction of a price movement for most currency pairs. As an illustration, when the exchange rate of EUR/USD shifts from 1.1205 to 1.1206, it has experienced a one-pip movement. There is an exception when it comes to currency pairs that involve the Japanese Yen. In this case, a pip corresponds to 0.01. Points are typically utilized to denote minor price fluctuations, especially in the futures market, and represent a fraction of a pip.

The term "point" can differ across markets, but it generally denotes the smallest price change before the decimal point.

Spreads: The spread represents the variance between the bid and ask price of a forex pair. It is an essential expense for traders in the Forex market and a crucial factor in successful trading. More liquidity and lower trading costs are often indicated by tighter spreads. On the other hand, a wide spread indicates reduced liquidity and increased trading expenses. The spreads can fluctuate significantly based on the currency pair, prevailing market conditions, and the specific time of day.

Having a solid grasp of how to analyze and interpret Forex quotes is crucial for traders to make well-informed decisions. Through a deep understanding of bid and ask prices, pips, and spreads, traders can effectively navigate their market entries and exits, increasing the likelihood of achieving successful trading outcomes.

CHAPTER 5

FUNDAMENTAL CONCEPTS IN FOREX

Base and Quote Currencies

Two currencies are always involved in every forex transaction, known as the currency pair. In a currency pair, the base currency is the first one listed, while the quote currency is the second. In the EUR/USD pair, the base currency is the Euro, while the quote currency is the US Dollar. The forex quote reveals the amount of the quote currency required to acquire a single unit of the base currency. Grasping the significance of the base and quote currencies is crucial for traders and investors to visualize price fluctuations and estimate potential gains or losses.

Understanding Lot Size and Its Impact on Investments

Lot Size: In the world of forex trading, a "lot" is used to represent a standardized unit of trade.

Three main types of lot sizes **exist:**

Standard Lot: Represents a substantial amount of 100,000 units of the base currency.

Mini Lot: Includes 10,000 units of the base currency.

Micro Lot: Consists of 1,000 units of the base currency.

The size of your trades has a direct impact on the level of risk involved. As an example, a movement of one pip for a standard lot results in a $10 shift (depending on the currency pair), while the same pip movement for a micro lot leads to a $0.10 change. Thus, it is of utmost importance to carefully choose the lot size, as it will greatly influence your risk management approach and the overall amount of capital that is exposed to potential risks.

Understanding Leverage and Margin

Leverage: Leverage in forex allows traders to control a large amount of currency using very little of their own money. It functions as a loan offered by the broker to the trader, allowing the trader to open a significantly larger position than they could with their own funds alone. As an expert in the field, I can illustrate the power of leverage by demonstrating how you can control a significant amount of money in the market with a relatively small investment. For instance, with a leverage ratio of 100:1, you have the ability to command $100,000 in the market while only using $1,000 of your own funds. Margin: This is the amount of money needed to open a leveraged position, or the money set aside as a deposit to hold a position.

Margin is directly tied to leverage. For example, if a broker mandates a 1% margin, it implies that you must have 1% of the trade's total value in your account to initiate a position. It serves as a form of security for the trade and is utilized to offset potential losses in case the market goes against you.

It is crucial to have a clear understanding of how leverage and margin function, as they have the potential to significantly increase both profits and losses. Traders must exercise caution when utilizing leverage and carefully handle their margin requirements to effectively maintain their positions and prevent margin calls. These calls are triggered when your account balance drops below the necessary margin level.

Understanding these core principles in forex—such as the base and quote currencies, lot size, and leverage and margin—empowers traders to effectively navigate the forex market, mitigate risk, and enhance their trading strategies for more favorable results.

CHAPTER 6

HOW FOREX TRADING WORKS

The Mechanics of Forex Trading

Trading in the forex market requires exchanging different currencies, anticipating price fluctuations to make profitable transactions. The mechanics of Forex trading are driven by the forces of supply and demand. When a specific currency is highly sought after, its value will increase in comparison to other currencies, while its value will decrease when its demand is low.

The global foreign exchange market operates around the clock, providing traders worldwide with the opportunity to engage in trading activities during the overlapping hours of international markets. Transactions occur at major financial hubs like London, New York, and Tokyo, making Forex an incredibly accessible and liquid financial market.

Executing a Forex Trade

To execute a Forex trade, adhere to the following instructions:

Select a Currency Pair: Determine the currency pair you wish to trade by conducting a thorough analysis of the market and making accurate predictions.

Choose the Type of Trade: Decide whether you want to purchase or sell the pair based on your assessment of whether the base currency will gain or lose strength against the quote currency.

Choose the size of your lot: Select the number of lots you wish to trade, taking into consideration that the size of the lot will impact the level of risk associated with your trade.

Consider Utilizing Leverage: Take into account the level of leverage you wish to employ, keeping in mind that although leverage can enhance your profit potential, it also amplifies your risk.

Establish Stop Loss and Take Profit Levels: These tools are essential for managing risk and determining when to exit trades, whether they result in losses or gains.

Execute the Trade: Once all parameters are in place, you can easily place your order using your trading platform. The trade will then be executed based on the conditions you have specified.

Exploring Different Order Types

The various types of orders in Forex trading play a crucial role in managing your trades and can have a significant impact on your overall trading strategy. Here are a few popular types:

Market Order: This type of order allows you to buy or sell a currency pair at the current market price, ensuring you get the best available rate. It is executed promptly and proves valuable when the swiftness of execution takes precedence over the price at which the order will be filled.

Limit Order: This order allows you to set a specific price at which you want to buy or sell a currency, ensuring that you get the best possible deal. An order to buy at a specific price can only be executed at that price or lower, while an order to sell at a specific price can be executed at that price or higher. This strategy is employed when there is an anticipation of the market reversing once it reaches the price that has been specified.

Stop-Loss Order: Its purpose is to minimize potential losses for investors when holding a position in a security. When placing a buy order, it's important to set the stop-loss order below the current market price. On the other hand, for a sell order, it's advisable to place the stop-loss order above the current market price.

Profit Locking Order: Comparable to a stop-loss, this order is employed to secure profits by automatically closing the trade once the price reaches a predetermined level of profit.

Stop-Entry Order: This is placed to buy above the market or sell below the market at a certain price. It is employed when there is an expectation that the price will persist in its current direction following a specific level being reached.

Having a solid grasp of trade placement and order types is essential for successfully navigating the Forex market. These tools enable traders to effectively manage their investments and minimize risks, ultimately maximizing their potential for profitability.

CHAPTER 7

ANALYZING THE FOREX MARKET

Fundamental Analysis

When it comes to Forex, one important aspect is to analyze the fundamental factors that impact the value of currencies. This involves carefully evaluating the economic conditions that play a role in determining their worth. This involves analyzing economic indicators, government policies, societal factors, and any events that could impact supply and demand. The objective is to ascertain the genuine worth of a currency and anticipate forthcoming fluctuations.

Key Economic Indicators

These reports and statistics are published by government or private sectors to provide insights into the economic conditions within a country. Some commonly used indicators are:

GDP (Gross Domestic Product): Represents the total market value of all final goods and services produced in a country and is a primary indicator of economic health.

Employment Data: High employment rates often lead to higher consumer spending and economic growth, which are bullish for the currency.

Trade Balance: A favorable trade balance, where exports

exceed imports, usually has a positive impact on a currency's strength. Conversely, a trade deficit can potentially weaken it.

Interest rates: The interest rates established by central banks, like the Federal Reserve in the U.S. or the European Central Bank in Europe, play a vital role in Forex trading. Higher interest rates provide lenders in an economy with a greater return compared to other nations. Consequently, when interest rates are increased, foreign capital is drawn in and this leads to an increase in the exchange rate. The opposite holds for countries with lower interest rates.

Economic Theories That Drive Forex

There are several economic theories that shed light on the

factors influencing currency rates and the reasons behind their constant fluctuations:

Purchasing Power Parity (PPP) indicates that the prices of goods in various countries should be the same when measured in a common currency.

Interest Rate Parity suggests that the exchange rate between currencies is influenced by the disparity in national interest rates for financial securities and deposits.

Balance of Payments Model: States that exchange rate should adjust to account for imbalances in a country's international payments for goods, services, and financial assets.

Technical Analysis

Technical analysis focuses on analyzing historical market data, particularly price and volume, using statistical methods. Technical analysts rely on past patterns to forecast future price movements, operating under the belief that history has a tendency to repeat itself.

Different Types of Charts

Line charts display the closing prices for each time period, offering a straightforward perspective on market trends.

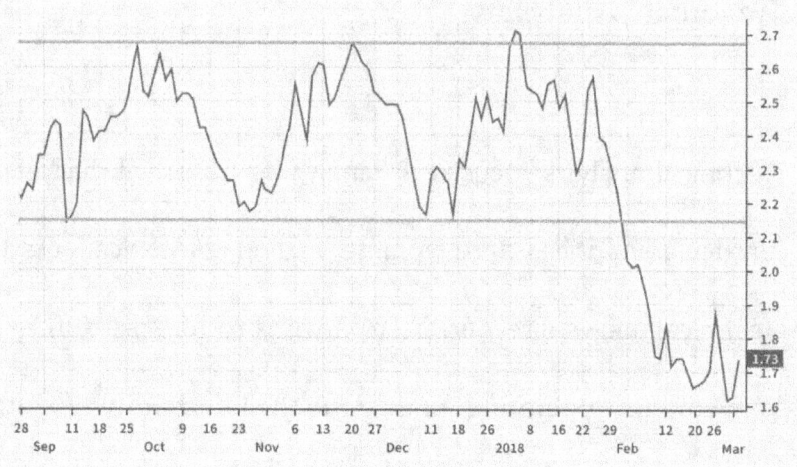

Bar Charts: Offer additional data, encompassing the opening, high, low, and closing prices for each period.

Candlestick Charts: Like bar charts, they offer a more visual way to depict price movements, displaying the direction of movement and the trading range.

Important Technical Indicators

Moving Averages: Reflect the average price within a specific time frame across multiple intervals. They help to smooth out price data in order to identify the direction of the trend.

RSI (Relative Strength Index) is a tool used to assess

overbought or oversold conditions by measuring the speed and change of price movements.

MACD (Moving Average Convergence Divergence): An indicator that shows the relationship between two moving averages and can signal changes in trend.

Understanding Support and Resistance

Support: A level where a downtrend may temporarily halt as demand becomes more concentrated.

Resistance: A level at which a trend can pause or rebound due to a concentration of selling interest.

Through the use of fundamental and technical analysis, traders can develop a well-rounded understanding of market conditions, enabling them to make more informed trading decisions. This chapter aims to establish a strong base for comprehending the analysis of the Forex market through the utilization of various tools and theories.

CHAPTER 8

DEVELOPING A TRADING PLAN

Importance of Having a Trading Plan

A trading plan serves as a detailed guide for traders, outlining the specifics of what, how, and when to trade, tailored to individual financial objectives, risk tolerance, and available capital. It serves as a trusted advisor to help maintain consistency, objectivity, and accountability in trading, which greatly enhances the chances of achieving profitable results. Having a well-thought-out strategy is crucial for traders to avoid making impulsive decisions driven by emotions, ultimately preventing costly mistakes.

Components of an Effective Trading Strategy

Setting Trading Goals: Clearly outline your desired outcomes in trading, whether it's a specific financial target or the enhancement of your trading abilities. It is important to set goals that are specific, measurable, achievable, relevant, and time-bound (SMART).

Risk/Reward Ratio: Decide on the risk/reward parameters for each trade. A popular approach is to target a risk/reward ratio that ensures the potential reward is at least double the potential risk.

Criteria for Entering and Exiting Trades: Provide clear guidelines for when to enter and exit trades. Various factors can be considered, such as technical indicators, specific events, or price patterns.

Money Management Rules: Determine the amount of your overall capital that you are comfortable risking on a single trade. Many experienced traders choose to allocate a small percentage of their capital to each trade.

Market Analysis: Discuss the approaches you will employ to analyze the market, whether it's through fundamental analysis, technical analysis, or a combination of both.

Effective Record Keeping: Implement a comprehensive system for documenting and analyzing each trade, enabling you to constantly improve your strategy and gain insights from previous trades.

Risk Management Strategies

Stop-Loss Orders: Utilize stop-loss orders to automatically close a trade at a predetermined price level, thus limiting potential losses.

Position Sizing: Determine the appropriate size of your position by considering your risk tolerance and the level of volatility in the currency pair you are trading.

Embrace diversification: Allocate your capital across various trades and strategies to mitigate risk. It is advisable to diversify your capital across different currency pairs or trades.

Effective Management of Leverage: Exercise caution

when using leverage. Using high leverage in trading can amplify potential gains, but it also carries the risk of substantial losses. It is important to exercise caution when utilizing leverage, ensuring that it remains at a reasonable level in relation to your total trading capital.

Consistent Evaluations: It is important to consistently evaluate your trading plan and strategies, particularly following a string of losses, major news events, or shifts in market conditions. This assists in adjusting and enhancing your trading strategy as time progresses.

Creating a well-thought-out trading plan is essential for individuals who are determined to achieve success in forex trading. It is beneficial to stay focused and composed when dealing with market fluctuations and emotional pressures. A carefully constructed strategy not only outlines your trading approach but also strengthens your capacity to assess previous results for ongoing enhancement.

CHAPTER 9

COMMON FOREX TRADING STRATEGIES

Exploring the World of Forex Day Trading

Day trading entails the purchase and sale of currency pairs within a single trading day. Traders take advantage of slight price fluctuations and use leverage to maximize profits from even the smallest changes in rates. Here are important aspects to consider when engaging in day trading:

Market Hours: Focus on trading during the most active hours when liquidity is highest, typically when major market sessions overlap (such as London and New York).

Speed and Precision: Day traders need to react quickly to market changes, which require efficient trading platforms and tools for real-time analysis.

Risk Management: Given the high number of trades, it's vital to use strict stop-loss orders and manage risks meticulously to avoid significant losses on a single trade.

Technical Analysis: This strategy relies heavily on technical analysis and indicators to make trading decisions due to the short timeframe of trades.

Effective Strategies for Swing Trading

Swing trading is ideal for individuals who are able to maintain positions for multiple days in order to take advantage of anticipated market fluctuations, whether they are upward or downward. Important elements consist of:

Timing: Unlike day traders, swing traders hold positions for several days or weeks, which mean they don't need to constantly monitor the market.

Technical and Fundamental Analysis: Swing traders frequently utilize a blend of technical and fundamental analysis to pinpoint possible trading prospects. Technical analysis may be utilized to determine optimal entry and exit points for trades, while fundamental analysis can provide insights into the broader market trends.

Risk Tolerance: Swing trading requires careful consideration of overnight holding costs and the possibility of market fluctuations, necessitating a comprehensive risk management approach.

Persistence and Patience: Achieving success in swing trading demands the ability to persistently wait for opportune trades and the patience to navigate through potential downturns.

Position Trading: Embracing a Strategic Approach

Position trading entails maintaining positions for a significant duration, spanning from several weeks to years, in order to capitalize on significant fluctuations in currency values. It is less influenced by short-term market fluctuations and generally emphasizes the broader economic fundamentals that drive currency trends. Here are some notable traits:

Fundamental Focus: Position traders often rely on fundamental analysis to make their trading decisions, looking at long-term economic trends and financial factors.

Market Sentiment and Trends: Gaining insights into and accurately forecasting long-term market trends are essential, necessitating a comprehensive analysis of geopolitical events, macroeconomic trends, and central bank rate decisions.

Managing Risk: The strategies involve utilizing lower leverage and wider stop-loss margins to account for extended exposure and the possibility of significant volatility.

Resilience: This strategy demands a considerable amount of resilience and a high tolerance for market corrections that may not impact the long-term trend.

Every trading strategy is designed to suit the needs of various traders, taking into account factors such as their risk tolerance, available capital, preferred trading time frame, and desired level of market involvement. By grasping and implementing these strategies successfully, traders can enhance their approaches according to their personal trading preferences and goals.

CHAPTER 10

TOOLS OF THE TRADE

Forex Trading Platforms

Forex trading platforms provide investors and traders with the necessary tools to open, close, and manage market positions. There are various types of platforms available; each designed to cater to different trading styles and preferences:

MetaTrader 4 and 5 (MT4/MT5): These platforms have gained worldwide recognition for their powerful features, intuitive interface, and comprehensive support for automated trading.

cTrader: Renowned for its user-friendly interface and sophisticated trading features, cTrader is highly favored by experienced traders due to its comprehensive charting options, transparent pricing, and extensive range of order types.

NinjaTrader: This platform is highly regarded by traders in the futures and forex markets who value its advanced charting and analysis tools. It is particularly favored by those who seek precision and comprehensive technical analysis capabilities.

Thinkorswim: Offered by TD Ameritrade, this platform is ideal for experienced traders who seek up-to-the-minute data feeds, advanced technical indicators, and real-time analysis.

Tools for Analysis

Having access to analytical tools is crucial for successful forex trading. These tools enable traders to analyze market data and economic information, allowing them to make informed predictions about future price movements. Useful tools to consider:

Economic Calendars: Track economic indicators and news releases that impact the forex market, crucial for planning trades around major events.

Charting Software: Traders can utilize tools with advanced charting capabilities to visualize data using a variety of technical indicators and graphical objects, enabling them to analyze trends effectively.

Exploring Technical Indicators and Oscillators: By utilizing various technical analysis tools such as MACD, RSI, Fibonacci retracements, and Bollinger Bands, traders can effectively analyze market trends, gauge volatility levels, and make predictions about future price movements using past data.

Sentiment indicators offer valuable insights into market dynamics, allowing traders to assess the possibility of trend reversals or continuations.

A computerized Trading Systems

Also referred to as algorithmic trading, automated trading systems enable traders to set precise rules for entering and exiting trades. Once these rules are programmed, they can be automatically executed by a computer. Advantages and factors to consider include:

Efficiency: Trades are executed at the best possible prices without delay.

Discipline: Automated systems reduce the emotional component of trading, particularly useful during volatile markets.

Backtesting: Traders can use historical data to evaluate the viability of a trading strategy before risking capital.

Over-Optimization: While backtesting strategies, it's crucial to avoid complex models that can be perfect on paper but fail in live trading.

Automated trading systems require careful monitoring and understanding as market conditions can change rapidly, impacting the effectiveness of the strategy. It is crucial for traders to have a clear understanding of how these systems work and the potential risks involved, including the possibility of technological failures.

By utilizing the appropriate trading platforms, analytical tools, and automated systems, traders can greatly improve their capacity to make well-informed decisions and effectively handle their trades. This chapter offers a comprehensive look at the essential tools that all traders should consider integrating into their trading strategy.

CHAPTER 11

UNDERSTANDING THE PSYCHOLOGY OF TRADING

Understanding the Psychological Factors in Trading

Engaging in trading involves more than just the application of knowledge and skills; it also encompasses a significant emotional aspect. Emotions have a substantial impact on trading decisions, often in a negative way. Traders often experience a range of emotions, including fear, greed, and hope. These emotions can sometimes cloud judgment and result in irrational decisions, such as holding onto losing positions for too long or exiting winning positions prematurely.

Recognizing and effectively handling these emotional aspects is vital for maintaining objectivity and discipline in trading.

Psychological Factors Impacting Forex Traders

There are various cognitive biases that can impact decision-making and ultimately influence trading outcomes. Some biases to consider are:

Overconfidence Bias: This arises when traders possess an exaggerated sense of confidence in their trading abilities or the reliability of their forecasts, often resulting in increased levels of risk-taking.

Confirmation Bias: Traders may tend to favor information that aligns with their existing beliefs or predictions, while potentially disregarding contradictory evidence.

Loss Aversion: Traders frequently experience the discomfort of losses more intensely than the satisfaction of an equal gain. This can result in cautious behavior that restricts potential profits.

Anchoring Bias: Traders often place excessive reliance on the first piece of information they receive, such as an initial price. This can lead to inaccurate trading decisions.

Building Mental Discipline

Building strong mental discipline is crucial for successfully navigating the emotional challenges and biases that come with trading. Important strategies to consider are:

Establishing Clear Objectives: Clearly outline your desired outcomes for your trading endeavors, encompassing both financial aspirations and personal growth targets.

Developing and adhering to a well-structured trading strategy: Having a carefully crafted trading plan is crucial for reducing impulsive decisions and maintaining a consistent trading approach.

Effective Stress Management: Discover powerful techniques to effectively manage and reduce stress. Engaging in activities beyond trading, like maintaining a regular exercise routine, practicing meditation, or pursuing hobbies that promote relaxation, can be beneficial.

Consistent Evaluation and Contemplation: Regularly analyze your trades to recognize behavioral patterns that may enhance or impede your performance. Reflecting on past experiences can be a valuable learning opportunity, allowing you to gain insights and prevent the recurrence of any errors.

Maintaining a Trading Journal: Recording your trades and the reasoning behind them can offer valuable insights into the emotional factors that influence your trading.

Recognizing and tackling the psychological aspects of trading is just as crucial as honing technical expertise. Developing strong mental discipline and emotional control is crucial for traders looking to navigate the forex market successfully. It is important to prioritize trading psychology as a key component of any comprehensive forex training program.

CHAPTER 12

NAVIGATING RISKS IN FOREX TRADING

Potential Risks Involved in Forex Trading

Trading in the Forex market can be highly lucrative, but it is crucial for traders to have a thorough understanding of the associated risks in order to effectively navigate their trading endeavors. There are several risks that need to be considered:

Market Risk: This refers to the potential for financial losses resulting from fluctuations in currency prices. The forex markets are known for their high volatility, which can lead to substantial losses when sudden shifts occur.

Risk of Leverage: Profits can be amplified through leverage, but it's important to note that it also heightens the possibility of substantial losses, particularly when a trade goes against you.

Interest rate risk: Fluctuations in interest rates have a direct impact on the strength of currencies and the prices in the forex market. It is important for traders to stay informed about central bank announcements and economic updates.

Risk of Limited Liquidity: Certain currency pairs may experience limited trading activity outside of regular market hours or during unusual market conditions, which could result in significant price discrepancies.

Political and Economic Risk: Various factors such as

political events, economic reports, and changes in government policy can lead to market instability, potentially resulting in unfavorable conditions.

Strategies to Mitigate Risks

To effectively handle the inherent risks of forex trading, traders have the option to implement a range of strategies:

Utilizing Stop-Loss Orders: Employing stop-loss orders can effectively mitigate potential losses by automatically closing a trade at a predetermined price level.

Appropriate Leverage Use: It is important to exercise caution when utilizing leverage as excessive use can result in significant financial losses. Gain a thorough understanding of leverage and adapt its usage according to your risk tolerance in your trading environment.

Understanding Risk/Reward Ratios: Prior to initiating a trade, it is crucial to assess the potential reward in relation to the associated risk. A popular approach is to identify situations where the potential gain outweighs the potential loss by a significant margin.

Diversification: Spread your risk by not putting all your capital into a single currency pair or trade.

Hedging: This strategy involves opening positions that can counterbalance any potential losses incurred by other positions. It's a sophisticated approach that can safeguard against unfavorable market shifts.

The Significance of Ongoing Education

Continuous learning is crucial in forex trading due to the ever-changing nature of the market. Keeping up-to-date with the latest techniques, market conditions, and economic trends can greatly improve a trader's decision-making abilities. Methods to encourage ongoing learning include:

Educational Resources: Utilize books, online courses, webinars, and seminars to keep abreast of new trading strategies and tools.

Economic Calendars and News Outlets: Stay informed about market events by regularly checking economic calendars and financial news outlets.

Simulation and Backtesting: Utilize demo accounts to refine trading strategies without any financial risk involved. Testing strategies against historical data is crucial for fine-tuning them prior to implementing them with actual funds.

Become part of trading communities: Engage in forums, trading communities, and workshops to connect with fellow traders and gain valuable insights into market dynamics.

By gaining a thorough understanding of the potential risks associated with forex trading and implementing proven risk management strategies, along with a continuous dedication to expanding knowledge, traders can enhance their likelihood of achieving success in the forex market. This chapter aims to assist new traders in navigating the intricate world of forex risk management and emphasizes the significance of education in developing a strong trading strategy.

CHAPTER 13

LEGAL AND REGULATORY ENVIRONMENT

Regulations for Forex Trading

The forex trading industry is closely monitored by regulatory bodies worldwide to ensure the prevention of fraud, the promotion of fair trading practices, and the protection of investor interests. Regulations differ from one country to another, but their main objective is to promote transparency and maintain the integrity of the marketplace. As an example:

In the United States, the forex market in the United States is regulated by the Commodity Futures Trading Commission (CFTC) and the National Futures Association (NFA). Registration with these organizations is a legal requirement for brokers to operate.

In the United Kingdom, the Financial Conduct Authority (FCA) oversees the industry, establishing guidelines for brokers to ensure they provide fair services to their clients.

Within the European Union, the Markets in Financial Instruments Directive (MiFID) establish the regulatory framework for financial services across all member states. Its objective is to enhance competition and safeguard consumers in the investment services sector.

It is essential to have a clear understanding of the regulations that are applicable in your jurisdiction and to ensure that your broker is fully compliant with these regulations. This is of utmost importance in order to trade securely and confidently.

Understanding Your Rights and Responsibilities

As a trader in the forex market, it is important to understand the rights and responsibilities that come with this role:

Rights: You have the right to transparent pricing, fair treatment from brokers, and access to your funds according to the terms of your account. You are entitled to receive information about the potential risks involved in trading activities and to maintain your privacy.

Responsibilities: It is your duty to accurately report and fulfill your tax obligations for your earnings. It is important to adhere to local regulations, have a clear understanding of the terms and conditions of your trading platform, and approach your trading activities with responsibility.

Protecting Yourself from Scams and Frauds

The forex market, given its global reach and immense scale, tends to attract individuals who seek to take advantage of inexperienced traders. To ensure your safety, take into account the following suggestions:

Verify Broker Credentials: Ensure that your broker is legitimately registered with and regulated by a reputable financial authority.

Be Wary of Unrealistic Promises: Be cautious of anyone

promising guaranteed returns or risk-free trading. These are typical indications of fraudulent activities.

Research Thoroughly: Before committing to any broker or service, thoroughly research their track record, read reviews, and check regulatory body websites for any warnings.

Use Secure and Transparent Payment Methods: It is advisable to steer clear of brokers who demand payment through untraceable methods. Reputable brokers provide a range of trusted and secure payment options.

Educate Yourself Continuously: Having a good understanding of the subject matter can greatly reduce the chances of being deceived by fraudulent activities. Make the most of the educational resources and ongoing training provided by trusted sources.

Legal Remedies and Procedures for Addressing Complaints

Learn the necessary steps to take if you encounter a scam or if a broker infringes upon your rights. This may require filing complaints with the appropriate financial authority, pursuing arbitration, or resorting to legal measures. Understanding these procedures can give you the knowledge you need to make informed decisions and safeguard your investments.

Understanding and adhering to the legal and regulatory requirements is crucial to safeguarding the integrity of your trading endeavors and your financial assets. This chapter provides traders with the necessary knowledge to identify legal standards and regulatory practices on a global scale. It also helps traders understand their rights and obligations, enabling them to take proactive measures to protect themselves from frauds and scams.

APPENDIX

To support beginners in the Forex market, providing a range of quick references and support materials can be highly beneficial. Here's a curated list of resources that can help new traders develop their understanding and skills:

Online Courses

1. **Babypips:** A well-known free online learning resource that provides comprehensive lessons on forex trading basics.

2. **Udemy:** Offers a variety of courses on forex trading for all levels, typically at a low cost.

3. **Coursera and EdX:** Provide courses from universities and colleges around the world, including finance and trading courses.

4. To access our online course after purchasing this book send an email to:

Exploitnneka@gmail.com

Websites

1. **Investopedia:** Offers a wealth of articles and tutorials on all aspects of forex trading and financial markets.

2. **Forex Factory:** Provides high-quality information including forex news, market analysis, and trading calendars.

3. **DailyFX:** Offers real-time forex news and analysis at the beginner and intermediate levels.

Tools

1. **Economic Calendars:** Track important economic announcements with calendars from websites like Forex Factory, Bloomberg, or Investing.com.

2. **Demo Accounts:** Most online forex brokers offer demo accounts where you can practice trading without risking real money.

3. **Trading Platforms:** MetaTrader 4 or 5 (MT4/5), cTrader, and NinjaTrader are popular platforms that provide valuable analytical tools and automated trading capabilities.

Forums and Social Media

1. **Forex Reddit Community (r/Forex):** A place to discuss trading, share strategies, and receive feedback from other traders.

2. **Trading View:** Social network for traders with tools for learning and sharing within the trading community.

3. **Bloomberg Market Concepts (BMC):** An online course that provides a comprehensive introduction to the financial markets.

Mobile Apps

1. **Thinkorswim:** Offers robust features for analysis, trading, and risk management on the go.

2. **FXStreet:** Provides forex news, real-time quotes, charts, and economic calendar.

3. **Bloomberg Business Mobile App:** A leading source for global business and financial news.

Using these resources, beginners can gain a solid foundation in forex trading, understand market dynamics, and develop the skills necessary for successful trading. It's recommended to start with learning the basics and gradually incorporate more advanced materials and tools as your understanding deepens.

EPILOGUE

As we draw the curtains on this guide, "Forex Trading Fundamentals; Understanding Basics of Forex Markets, Currency Pairs and How Forex Trading Works," it is important to reflect on the journey we've embarked on together. Through these pages, we've delved deep into the intricacies of the Forex market—from the basic concepts that govern currency trading to the more sophisticated strategies that can help you navigate this dynamic arena.

Forex trading offers a unique set of challenges and opportunities; it is a field where fortunes can be made and, just as easily, lost. The journey to becoming a proficient Forex trader is continuous and ever-evolving. Markets change and economic scenarios shift, necessitating an adaptable and informed approach to trading.

Looking Ahead

The road ahead in Forex trading is as promising as it is daunting. New technologies and evolving financial regulations continuously reshape the landscape in which we operate. To stay ahead, a commitment to ongoing education and adaptation is imperative. Utilize the tools, strategies, and frameworks discussed in this book as your foundational guide, but remain vigilant and proactive about expanding your knowledge and refining your techniques.

Embracing Continuous Improvement

Your growth as a Forex trader depends not only on the strategies you employ but also on your mindset. Embrace both your successes and failures as vital learning opportunities. Keep a detailed trading journal, review your performance regularly, and stay engaged with the trading community to exchange insights and experiences. This approach will not only enhance your skills but also deepen your understanding of market dynamics.

The Role of Persistence

Persistence is key in Forex trading. The path is often strewn with challenges, and the market's volatility can test even the most seasoned traders. Remember, every trader has had their share of losses; it is resilience and continued learning that set successful traders apart.

Final Thoughts

As you move forward, consider this book not just as a read-through guide but as a companion in your Forex trading journey. Revisit chapters, explore concepts with fresh eyes, and keep pace with the global economic environment. The strategies and insights offered here are meant to equip you with the knowledge to begin or enhance your trading journey, but they are just the starting point.

May your trading path be prudent, your decisions informed, and your ventures prosperous. Here's to achieving your financial goals through Forex trading—may it be a rewarding and enlightening journey.

Wishing you success on the trading floor and beyond

NOTE TO FX TRADERS

Dear FX Trader,

Thank you for choosing "Forex Trading Fundamentals; Understanding Basics of Forex Markets, Currency Pairs and How Forex Trading Works." We hope that this book serves as a solid foundation in your Forex trading education and that the strategies and insights within these pages empower you on your trading journey.

As you apply the knowledge you've gained, remember that this is just the beginning. The world of Forex is vast and complex, offering endless opportunities for growth and success. To further support your development as a Forex trader, we are excited to announce that this book is the first in a series designed to explore the Forex market in even greater depth.

In our upcoming volumes, we will delve into advanced trading techniques and exploit strategies that go beyond the basics, providing you with more sophisticated tools and insights that can help you maximize your trading potential. These future books will build on the foundational knowledge you've acquired here, guiding you through the intricacies of complex Forex strategies used by the most successful traders.

Keep an eye out for our next releases. We are eager to continue this journey with you, offering more insights and strategies to help you refine your trading skills and enhance your market understanding.

Thank you for your trust and commitment. We look forward to bringing you more valuable resources that will assist you in achieving your Forex trading aspirations.

Warm regards,

EXPLOIT KNOWLEDGE